SCHIRMER'S LIBRARY
OF MUSICAL CLASSICS

SERGEI RACHMANINOFF

Preludes
For the Piano

→ Op. 23 — 10 Preludes

Library Volume 1630

Op. 32 — 13 Preludes

Library Volume 1631

ISBN 978-0-7935-6498-9

G. SCHIRMER, Inc.

DISTRIBUTED BY

HAL•LEONARD®
CORPORATION
7777 W. BLUEMOUND RD. P.O. BOX 13819 MILWAUKEE, WI 53213

CONTENTS

39716

I

S. Rachmaninoff, Op. 23, № 1.

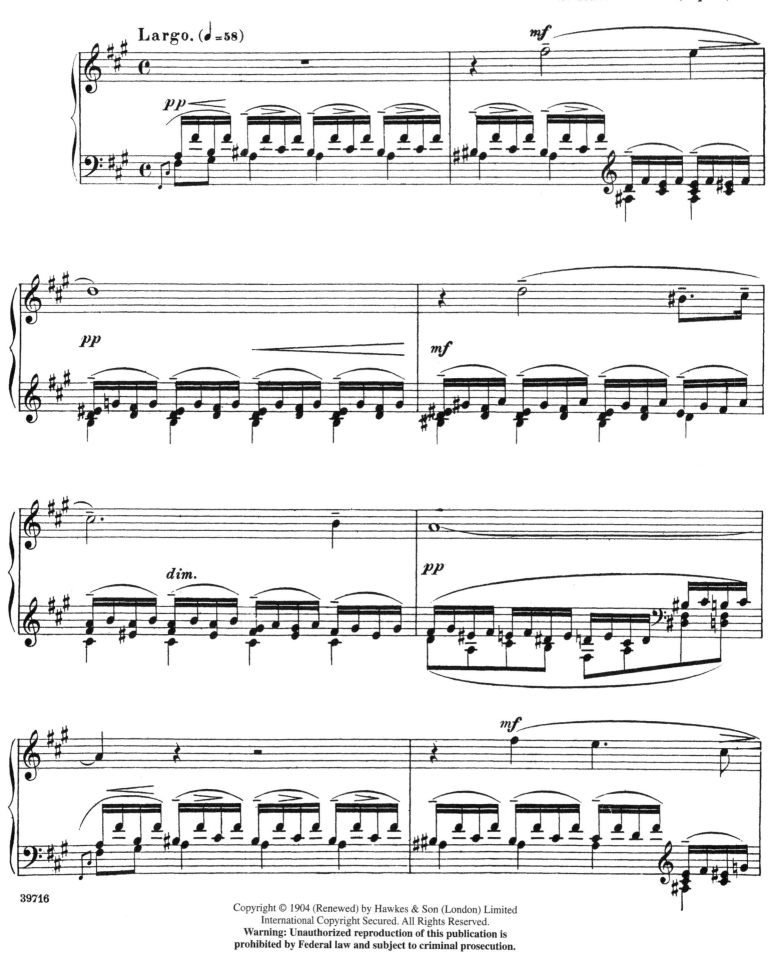

II

S. Rachmaninoff, Op. 23, N? 2

III

S. Rachmaninoff, Op. 23, No. 3.

Tempo di minuetto. (♩ = 66)

Un poco più mosso.

IV

S. Rachmaninoff, Op.23, No 4.

V

S. Rachmaninoff, Op. 23, № 5

Alla marcia. (♩=108)

Un poco meno mosso.

Tempo I.

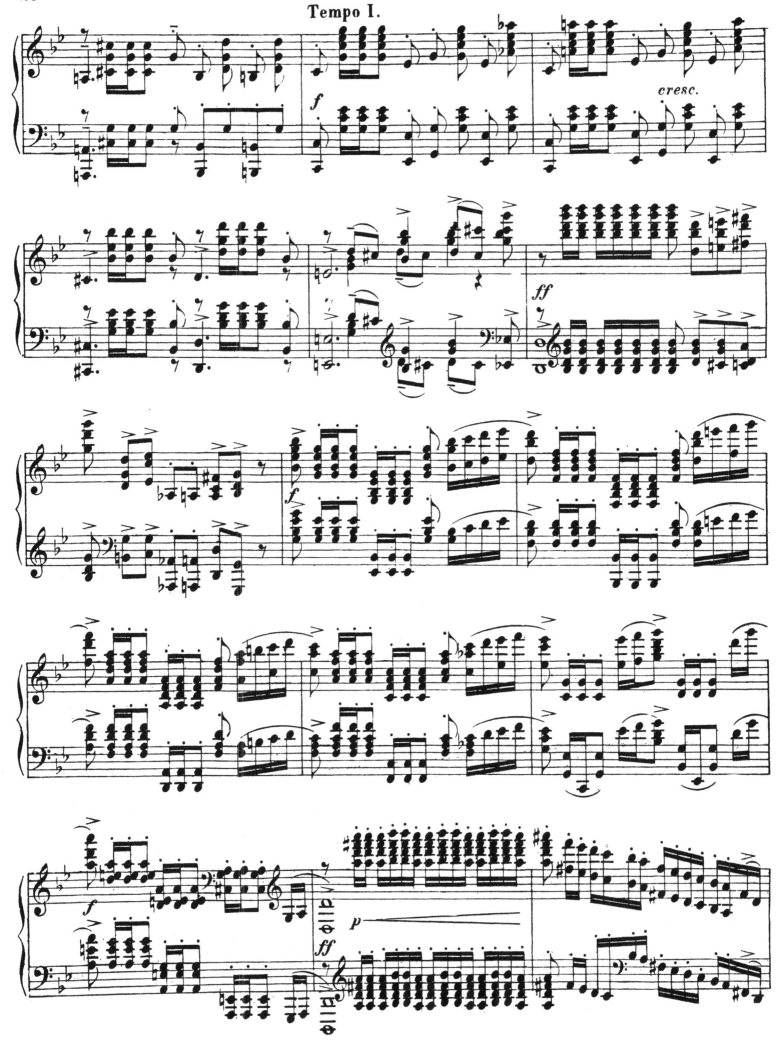

VI

S. Rachmaninoff, Op. 23, № 6.

Andante. (♩ = 72)

VII

S. Rachmaninoff, Op. 23. № 7.

VIII

S. Rachmaninoff, Op. 23, N.º 8.

39716

IX

S. Rachmaninoff, Op. 23, № 9.

Presto. (♩=152)

X

S. Rachmaninoff, Op. 23, № 10